Python for Data Science

Science

A Comprehensive guide to python Programming, Data Analytics, and Coding Essentials Tools

Andrew Park

Table of Contents

Introduction

Python is one of the top programming languages, universities and industries are preferring to teach it and use respectively. The charm of Python is hidden in the fact that it has extremely large applications in a wide range of fields. Most people abhor Python because of its use in building artificial intelligence models. They fear that these Python-powered AI models will drive people out of different industries and snatch their jobs. They quote the example of Tesla's driverless taxi program by which Tesla pretends to replace Uber's taxis in the US market. But the reality is different. In fact, Python-powered AI models will create many more jobs instead of removing jobs For example, building these models will become an independent industry. Also, the implementation of these AI models will become a new business sector.

Data science is going to take the corporate world by storm. Data science is based on Python programming language, as more and more companies are now moving in a neck-on-neck competition. All they crave is a way to take an edge over their competitors. They do each thing for power and to get ahead. In this regard, Python seems to be promising. Python-backed data science tends to equip industries with sophisticated data about past and present sales patterns, which can help corporate sector CEOs make wiser decisions about sales and development of marketing strategies.

The biggest advantage for learners of Python is that you don't have to compile the code. In C++, you have to compile the entire program first and then run it. Only then you will be able to see whether your program runs or returns an error. Python offers the same level of programming and even at a higher stage, but still, it is an interpreted language that can be easily written, edited, and corrected.

Python is very easy to read and learn. You can easily read source codes for different programs that are created by other programmers. But no matter how easy it is on the outside to read and learn, it needs, like all the other programming languages, dedicated practice. You will have to get to the Python editor and practice all codes. In the beginning, you can take the code and just paste it in the editor to see the results. In the second phase, you can make minor edits to the code and see the results. In the third phase, you will be able to completely reshape a program and see how it runs in the Python shell. Given the increasing applications of Python, learning it is extremely profitable from the angle of the global job market. Python can give you the much-needed edge over others when it comes to securing high paid jobs.

Chapter 1:   Python Installation

The up-to-date edition with the binaries, current source codes, documentation, latest news, etc. can be accessed at the official Python website: http://www.Python.org/

Here, you can download the documentation for Python from the site. It is accessible in various formats like PDF, HTML, and PostScript.

Python Documentation Website: www.Python.org/doc/

How to Install Python

Python Environment Variables:

Variable	Description
PYTHONPATH	It is similar to PATH. This variable foretells the Python interpreter as to where it can locate the module files that you can import into a program. PYTHONPATH must have a Python source library directory and the directories in

	which your Python code is present. PYTHONPATH is sometimes set by the Python installer automatically.
PYTHONSTARTUP	It has the path for the initialization file, which contains Python source codes that are executed every time you work on the interpreter. This file is often named .Pythonrc.py in Unix, which usually has commands that can load the utilities or can modify the PYTHONPATH.
PYTHONCASEOK	This is used in Windows OS for instructing Python to find case-insensitive matches in an import statement. You can set this to any random value for activating it.
PYTHONHOME	It is an alternative search path that is embedded in PYTHONSTARTUP or PYTHONPATH directories for switching the module libraries very easily.

Running Python

Python can be run on a system in three ways.

Interactive Interpreter

You can start by entering Python and then begin programming in its interpreter by beginning from the command line on any platform that provides a command line interpreter or a shell window.

A list of command line options is given in the table below.

Option	Description
-d	Provide the output after debugging
-O	Optimized byte code generation i.e. the .pyo file is generated
-S	Don't run the import site for searching Python paths in a startup.
-v	Details of the import statement
-X	Disable the class-based built-in exceptions
-c cmd	It runs Python script sent in cmd String
file	The python script is run from the given file

Script from Command-line

Calling an interpreter on your application can help you run and execute your Python script in the command line.

Integrated Development Environment (IDE)

It is possible to run Python from a GUI too. The one thing you require is a system that supports Python.

Chapter 2: Python Data Types

Python supports different data types. Each variable should belong to one of the data types supported in Python. The data type determines the value that can be assigned to a variable, the type of operation that may be applied to the variable as well as the amount of space assigned to the variable. Let's discuss different data types supported in Python.

Python Numbers

These data types help in the storage of numeric values. The creation of number-objects in Python is done after we have assigned a value to them. Consider the example given below:

```
total = 55
age = 26
```

The statement can be used for the deletion of single or multiple variables. This is shown below:

```
del total
del total, age
```

In the first statement, we are deleting a single variable while in the second statement, we are deleting two variables. If the variables to be deleted are more than two, separate them by using a comma and they will be deleted.

In Python, there are four numerical values which are supported:

- Int
- Float
- Complex

In Python 3, all integers are represented in the form of long integers.

The Python integer literals belong to the int class.

Example

Run the following statements consecutively on the Python interactive interpreter:

```
x=10
x
```

You can run it on the Python interactive interpreter and you will observe the following:

The float is used for storing numeric values with a decimal point.

Example

```
x=10.345
x
```

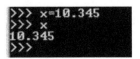

If you are performing an operation with one of the operands being a float and the other being an integer, the result will be a float.

Example

```
5 * 1.5
```

As shown above, the result of the operation is 7.5, which is a float.

Complex numbers are made of real and imaginary parts, with the imaginary part being denoted using a j. They can be defined as follows:

```
x = 4 + 5j
```

In the above example, 4 is the real part, while 5 is the imaginary part.

In Python, there is a function named type() that can be used for determining the type of a variable. You only have to pass the name of the variable inside that function as the argument and its type will be printed.

Example

```
x=10
type(x)
```

```
>>> x=10
>>> type(x)
<class 'int'>
>>>
```

The variable x is of int class as shown above. You can try it for other variable types as shown below:

```
name='nicholas'
type(name)
```

```
>>> name='nicholas'
>>> type(name)
<class 'str'>
>>>
```

The variable is of the string class as shown above.

Python Strings

Python strings are a series of characters enclosed within

quotes. Use any type of quotes to enclose Python strings, that is, either single, double, or triple quotes. To access string elements, we use the slice operator. String characters begin at index 0, meaning that the first character string is at index 0. This is good when you need to access string characters. To concatenate strings in Python, we use the + operator, the asterisk 9 *) is used for repetition.

Example

```
#!usrbin/Python3
thanks = 'Thank You'
print (thanks) # to print the complete string
print (thanks[0]) # to print the first character of the
string
print (thanks[2:7]) # to print the 3rd to the 7th
character of the string
print (thanks[4:]) # to print from the 5th character of
the string
print (thanks * 2) # to print the string two times
print (thanks + "\tAgain!") # to print a concatenated
string
```

The program prints the following once executed:

```
Thank You
T
ank Y
k You
Thank YouThank You
Thank You  Again!
```

Notice that we have text beginning with the # symbol. The symbol denotes the beginning of a comment. The Python print will not act on the text from the symbol to the end of the line. Comments are meant at enhancing the readability of code by giving explanations. We defined a string named thanks with the value Thank You. The print (thanks[0]) statement helps us access the first character of the string; hence it prints T. You also notice that the space between the two words is counted as a character.

Chapter 3:   Python Variables

Understanding Python variables, classes, and how to operate is essential for both beginners and programmers who intend to expand their programming skills.

What Is A Variable in Python?

When writing complex codes, your program will demand data essential to conduct changes when you proceed with your executions. Variables are, therefore, sections used to store code values created after you assign a value during program development. Python, unlike other related language programming software, lacks the command to declare a variable as they change after being set. Besides, Python values are undefined like in most cases of programming in other computer languages.

Variation in Python is therefore described as memory reserves used for storing data values. As such, Python variables act as storage units, which feed the computer with the necessary data for processing. Each value comprises of its database in Python programming, and every data are categorized as Numbers, Tuple, Dictionary, and List, among others. As a programmer, you understand how variables work and how helpful they are in creating an effective program using Python. As such, the tutorial will enable learners to understand declare, re-declare, and concatenate, local and global variables as well as how to delete a variable.

Variables vs. Constants

Variables and constants are components used in Python programming but perform different functions. Variables, as well as constants, utilize values used to create codes to execute during program creation. Variables act as essential storage locations for data in the memory, while constants are variables whose value remains unchanged. In comparison, variables store reserves for data while constants are a type of variable files with consistent values written in capital letters and separated by underscores.

Variables vs. Literals

Literal is a raw data given in a variable or constant. In Python, there are various types of literals: Numeric, String, and Boolean. There are also Literal collections such as Tuple, Dict, List, and Set.

Both Variables and Literals deal with unprocessed data. The difference is that Variables store them.

```
foo = 42

 ^       ^

 |       |--- literal, 42 is *literally* 42
```

```
|
|--variable "foo", and the content may vary (is
variable)
```

Variables vs. Arrays

Python variables have a unique feature where they only name
the values and store them in the memory for quick retrieval
and supplying the values when needed. On the other hand,
Python arrays or collections are data types used in
programming language and categorized into list, tuple, set,
and dictionary, which will be discussed later. When
compared to variables, the array tends to provide a platform
to include collective functions when written while variables
store all kinds of data intended. When choosing your
charming collection, ensure you select the one that fits your
requirements henceforth meaning retention of meaning,
enhancing data security and efficiency.

Classifications of Python Arrays
Essential for Variables

Lists

Python lists offer changeable and ordered data and written
while accompanying square brackets, for example, "an
apple," "cherry." Accessing an already existing list by

referring to the index number while with the ability to write negative indexes such as '-1' or '-2'. You can also maneuver within your list and select a specific category of indexes by first determining your starting and endpoints. The return value with therefore be the range of specified items. You can also specify a scale of negative indexes, alter the value of the current item, loop between items on the list, add or remove items, and confirming if items are available.

Dictionaries

Python dictionaries comprise of indexed, changeable but unordered items typically written while with curly brackets with keys and values. Some of the activities involved include item access by use of a keyword inside the parentheses; conduct value changes, loop, check critical availability, length of the dictionary, and both adding and removing unwanted items. Besides, Python allows you to copy the dictionary by writing 'dict2 = dict1'. 'dict2' will become a representation to 'dict1' therefore makes any necessary changes automatically. Another way of creating a copy is also by using a built-in Dictionary technique, that is, 'copy.'

In other instances, Python dictionaries can also have other dictionaries within them a process referred to as nested dictionaries. You can readily determine the number of dictionaries present in the nest by creating three already available. You can also generate your dictionary through the 'dict()' contractor function. The function enables the copying of the previous dictionary or the creation of a completely new one. Within the Python dictionary, there exist several built-in techniques to implement and enjoy the efficiency of the dictionaries present.

Naming Variables

The naming of variables remains straightforward, and both beginners and experienced programmers can readily perform the process. However, providing titles to these variables accompany specific rules to ensure the provision of the right name. Consistency, style, and adhering to variable naming rules ensure that you create an excellent and reliable name to use both today and in the future. The rules are:

- Names must have a single word, that is, with no spaces
- Names must only comprise of letters and numbers as well as underscores such as (_)
- The first letter must never be a number
- Reserved words must never be used as variable names

When naming variables, you should bear in mind that the system is case-sensitive, hence avoid creating the same names within a single program to prevent confusion. Another important component when naming is considering the style.

It entails beginning the title with a lowercase letter while using underscores as spaces between your words or phrases used. Besides, the program customarily prevents starting the name with a capital letter. Begin with a lowercase letter and either mix or use them consistently.

When creating variable names, it may seem so easy, but sometimes it may become verbose henceforth becoming a disaster to beginners. However, the challenge of creating sophisticated names is quite beneficial for learned as it prepares you for the following tutorials. Similarly, Python enables you to write your desired name of any length consisting of lower- and upper-case letters, numbers as well as underscores. Python also offers the addition of complete Unicode support essential for Unicode features in variables.

As already discussed, specific rules are governing the procedure for naming variables; hence adhere to them to create an exceptional name for your variables. Create more readable names that have meaning to prevent instances of confusion to your members, especially programmers. A more descriptive name is much preferred compares to others. However, the technique of naming variables remains illegible as different programmers decide on how they are going to create their kind of names.

Methods of Creating a Multi-Name for Python Variables

- Pascal case: this method entails the first, second, and subsequent words in the name as capitalized to enhance readability. For example, ConcentrationOfWhiteSmoke.
- Camel case: the second and subsequent words of the name created remains capitalized. For example, ConcentrationofWhiteSmoke.
- Snake case: snake method of creating variable names entails a separator of words using an underscore as mentioned earlier. For example, concentration_of_white_smoke.

Learning Python Strings, Numbers and Tuple

Python strings are part of Python variables and comprise objects created from enclosing characters or values in double-quotes. For example, 'var = Hello World'. With Python not supporting character types in its functions, they are however treated as strings of one more characters as well as substrings. Within the Python program, there exist several string operators making it essential for variables to be named and stored in different formats. Some of the string operators commonly used in Python are [], [:], 'in', r/R, %, + and *.

There exist several methods of strings today. Some include replacing Python string () to return a copy of the previous value in a variable, changing the string format, that is, upper and lower cases and using the 'join' function, especially for concatenating variables. Other methods include the reverse function and split strings using the command 'word.split'. What to note is that strings play an important role, especially in naming and storage of values despite Python strings being immutable.

On the other hand, Python numbers are categorized into three main types; that is, int, float, and complex. Variable of numbers are usually created when assigning a value for them. For instance, int values are generally whole numbers with unlimited length and are either positive or negative such as 1, 2, and 3. Float numbers also either positive or negative and may have one or more decimals like 2.1, 4.3 and 1.1 while complex numbers comprise both of a letter 'j' as the imaginary portion and numbers, for example, 1j, -7j or 6j+5. As to verify the variable number is a string, you can readily use the function 'type().'

A collection of ordered values, which remain unchangeable, especially in Python variables, is referred to as a tuple. Python tuples are indicated with round brackets and available in different ways. Some useful in Python variables are access tuple items by index numbers and inside square brackets. Another is tuple remaining unchanged, especially after being created but provides a loop by using the function 'for.' And it readily encompasses both count and index methods of tuple operations.

Types of Data Variables

String

A text string is a type of data variable represented in either String data types or creating a string from a range of type char. The syntax for string data comprises multiple declarations including 'char Str1[15], 'char Str5[8] = "ardiono"; among others. As to declare a string effectively, add null character 'Str3', declare arrays of chars without utilizing in the form of 'Str1' and initialize a given array and leave space for a larger string such as Str6. Strings are usually displayed with doubles quotes despite the several versions available to construct strings for varying data types.

Char

Char are data types primarily used in variables to store character values with literal values written in single quotes, unlike strings. The values are stores in numbers form, but the specific encoding remains visibly suitable for performing arithmetic. For instance, you can see that it is saved as 'A' +, but it has a value of 66 as the ASCII 'A' value represents 66. Char data types are usually 8 bits, essential for character storage. Characters with larger volumes are stored in bytes. The syntax for this type of variable is 'char var = val'; where 'var' indicates variable name while 'val' represents the value assigned to the variable.

Byte

A byte is a data type necessary for storing 8-bit unsigned numbers that are between 0 to 255 and with a syntax of 'byte var = val;.' Like Char data type, 'var' represents variable name while 'val' stands for the value to he assigned that variable. The difference between char and byte is that char stores smaller characters and with a low space volume while byte stores values which are larger.

int

Another type of data type variable is the int, which stores 16-bit value yielding an array of between -32,768 and 32,767, which varies depending on the different programming platforms. Besides, int stores 2's complement math, which is negative numbers, henceforth providing the capability for the variable to store a wide range of values in one reserve. With

Python, this type of data variable storage enables transparency in arithmetic operations in an intended manner.

Unsigned int

Unsigned int also referred to, as unsigned integers are data types for storing up to 2 bytes of values but do not include negative numbers. The numbers are all positive with a range of 0 to 65,535 with Duo stores of up to 4 bytes for 32-byte values, which range from 0 to 4,294,967,195. In comparison, unsigned integers comprise positive values and have a much higher bit. However, ints take mostly negative values and have a lower bit hence store chapters with fewer values. The syntax for unsigned int is 'unsigned int var = val;' while an example code being 'unsigned int ledPin = 13;'

Float

Float data types are values with point numbers, that is to say, a number with a decimal point. Floating numbers usually indicate or estimate analog or continuous numbers, as they possess a more advanced resolution compared to integers. The numbers stored may range from the highest of 7.5162306E+38 and the lowest of -3.2095174E+38. Floating-point numbers remain stored in the form of 32 bits taking about 4 bytes per information fed.

Unsigned Long

This is data types of variables with an extended size; hence it stores values with larger storages compare to other data types. It stores up to 32 bits for 4 bytes and does not include negative numbers henceforth has a range of 0 to 4,294,967,295. The syntax for the unsigned long data type is 'unsigned long var = val;' essential for storing characters with much larger sizes.

Declaring Variables

As stated, variables are the naming and storing data values of both numerical and letters primarily used during Python programming. Before those values are used, they have to be declared to identify and perform the desired function in your program. Therefore, declaring a value means defining the type, and sometimes setting or initializing the value, though it remains optional but crucial. When creating your program, ensure you understand the extent of your variables by considering the scope of numbers you are storing. Excessive storage of values may result in rollovers, as the space used is insufficient.

The size of where to declare your values also affects a

programmer's outcome on created programs. The technique of selecting a specific storage unit influences the function of applications, especially when determining the codes. The scope henceforth is an essential aspect of declaring variables as it affects the results of your program. Another form is through initializing variables to decide on which value to start with during declaration. Initialized variables make it easy for programmers to readily choose a starting point when declaring or used for other purposes.

Creating and Declaring Variable

Python programs have limited access to a direct command to declare or create variables instantly. However, some essential rules may become a critical component for the process to occur. Besides, Python does not necessarily require data type specification but is created immediately when the value is assigned. When assigning values using Python, especially for complex or multiple assignments, it uses inferred language techniques, for instance, in detecting types of values assigned in a given variable.

Variables Assignment

Variables are neither declared nor defined when utilizing Python programming henceforth creation is quite straightforward. Creating a variable is simply assigning a value and begins using it. The process uses a single equal (=) symbol useful for statements and expressions. For example, creating n=38 in Python suggests that 'n' is assigned the value '38' and the value can be readily be substituted during programming.

Like literals values, the value used may be displayed directly by the interpreter without the use of 'print().' However, if you change the value, instead of 'n=38', the value will be substituted; for instance, if you input value 1000, it will display 'n=1000'. Python henceforth allows you to make changes where needed as well as the operation of chained assignments and input a similar value to different variables simultaneously. For example, a=b=c=d=38.

Re-Declaring Variables

After you have even declared a variable in Python, you can make changes by either declaring it again or assign a substitute value. That is, you can replace or connect a different value to the previous one readily through the re-declaration process. Re-declaring variables are beneficial as it enables you to accept user-generated codes to already existing values initialized. Similarly, you may wish to change the program or make some alterations during your project.

Reassigning variables are more vital for complicated or

extensive programs already incorporated by another programmer, and you are taking over. As such, you make significant changes in the declared values to enhance the effectiveness of your program is created. The Python interpreter plays a substantial role in discarding the original value and adding the new ones. The type of new values attached may either be different or comprise of unique identity when compared to the old ones.

For example, if your original value was 'x' and you need to change it to be an integer of '76', you first reassign 'x' to be a string, ass your new value and a replacement of the value immediately becomes a success. The example suggests that the value 'x' undergoes an assignment to the value of an integer and is later reassigned with the value of the string. Variable re-declare is most effective when you are aware of the readability of codes and with an object to create clear programs.

Concatenate Variables

If you wish to concatenate variables of several data types through Python, for instance, several variables and string variables, then you need to declare the values into strings. In case the number variables are not declared when concatenating different values, Python programming would stop and display TypeError indicating the procedure is unsuccessful. As to correct the situation, you will have to declare the number of variables as a string.

The process in Python programming is quite different compared to other programs like Java and C ++, which immediately concatenate several numbers without declaring them into strings. For instance, if you need to concatenate 'computer and '58', however when you declare the integer as a string, it can readily concatenate the two in the form of "computer + str(58) = computer58".

Global Variables

Global variables utilized in Python are a multipurpose variable used in any part of the world while anywhere. The variable used can operate in your program or module while in any part of the globe henceforth using values whenever you travel as a programmer. Global variables are useful for programmers to create their programs while moving from one location to another. Some of the benefits include variables that are used across function or module as well as it does not require re-declarations for performance.

When compared to local variables, global variables have an 'f' scope and assigned value 101, displayed as 'f=101', printed as an output. For example, when you re-declare a variable as a global variable in a given function, change it within the role and print it outside the task. The variable would provide a third party outcome useful globally. Therefore, global variables are found outside functions indicating that not all variables are readily accessed from anywhere globally. As a beginner, it is crucial to understand the difference between global and local variables to develop the necessary variables suitable for your programs.

Local Variables

Unlike global variables, local variables are used locally, declared within a Python function or module, and utilized solely in a specific program or Python module. When implemented outside particular modules or tasks, the Python interpreter will fail to recognize the units henceforth throwing an error message for undeclared values. Like global variables, local variables use the 'f' variable where it is declared to assume local scope and assigned 'I am learning Python' and then recognized as a local variable.

For example, when you declare the variable 'f' the second time, it changes to a new function and results in a local variable. As such, when you accept that variable in the inside function, the process will run without any problems. The execution is made possible as the second print(f) produces a value assigned to 'f' as Intellipaat. Whereas, when you print the value outside the function 'f', it results in a value assigned to it, which is outside the function, that is, a third print(f). In that case, local variables are used only in two surrounding environments of Python programming with those outside the function leading to failure of operations unless declared.

Using Variables

Immediately the variables are declared, they can be readily defined by setting those equal to the value you intend to store with the single same sign referred to as the assignment operator. The single equal sign, therefore, enables the program to put the desired variable either on the right or left side on whichever side. After seeding the variables, that is, assigned each variable with a value, test-specific values to determine if suits the program or use it directly.

For instance, you can use certain codes to test if the inputVariable2 is less than 50, thus set a delay time based on it with a minimum of 50. The example therefore tests the variable 'if (inputVariable2 <50)' and sets a given variable if it is successful 'inputVariable2 = 50' and delays the results using the function 'delay(inputVariable2)'. When using variables, ensure they have a more descriptive name for readability purposes. It also enables you, and someone else understands what the variable entails as well as recognition during the programming process.

Deleting Variables

On the other hand, if you make a mistake, get rid of your current project, or just doing away with everything, Python provides a useful feature to delete any variable and create more space for storage of other values. Similarly, there are some unwanted variables, and you wish to get rid of them, the delete variable is henceforth the choice for you. When deleting a variable, you should be cautious as to avoid deleting essential values within a variable. As such, ensure you know the name of the variable to delete.

If you are deleting a file with a variable name, which does not match, the Python interpreter typically throws an error message: 'NameError: name (filename) is not identified.' As to delete a variable effectively, there exists a command within the program; del 'variable name', and the variable will remove instantly. Ensure you input the correct name before running the command. As to confirm if your file is deleted, you may try to print, and if you see an error message, it indicates that the variable was deleted successfully.

Functions and Sets In Python Variables

There are minimal chances for a beginner to understand variables and the general operation of creating Python programs before understanding what are sets and functions as used in variables. When mentioning sets, objects, and functions, it means a different thing when it comes to computer programming. One of the most definitions of functions in variables is the set of related statements, values, and codes grouped and stored together to perform a particular task.

On the other hand, a set is a collective term to refer to Python data types with mutable free from duplication arranged in an unordered manner. Since you are learning about Python variables, understanding functions and sets contribute to familiarizing yourself with these terms; hence, you can easily interact with Python programming languages. Bear in mind that sets for had provided a particular index order of data while functions may not demand any input but solely executed when precisely needed.

Some of the standard features of sets include lack of a specific order of each value, number, code, and the item is unique, collections are immutable, and they offer modifications such as addition and deletion. The main advantage of utilizing sets in Python variables is that it optimizes the method of checking element is included in the right set or not. Also, it allows you to remove some aspects, but it only needs to be unique and immutable.

Functions make programs more manageable and organized mostly for programmers working on complicated tasks. Such tasks are with smaller and modular lumps of codes, thus increasing readability and reusability. As such, Python offers three types of functions; Python Built-in, user-defined and anonymous functions. The functions can only be initially named, written, and executed to perform a particular kind of input and create a desired program essential for both beginners and programmers.

Chapter 4:   Basic Operators of Python Language

Python is considered a high-level programming language with less complexity when it comes to using the basic operators in the code. It is built to read and implement computer language easily. Python provides various types of operators for performing tasks. Let's see the basic operators provided by Python.

Types of Operators

1. Python Arithmetic Operators
2. Python Assignment Operators
3. Python Comparison Operators
4. Python Logical Operators
5. Python Bitwise Operators
6. Python Membership Operators
7. Python Identity Operators

Python Arithmetic Operators

Arithmetic operators help us to solve several types of mathematical problems like addition, subtraction, multiplication, exponential values, floor divisions, etc. Let's suppose we have two variables whose values are x = 16, y = 4.

Operator	Description	Example
Addition (+)	This operator will be adding the values on both sides of operands.	x + y = 20
Subtraction (-)	This operator will be subtracting the right-hand side value from the left-hand side value of the operand.	x − y = 12
Multiplicatio n (*)	This operator will be multiplying the two values on both sides of the operands.	x * y = 64
Division (/)	This operator will be dividing the left-hand side value by the right-hand side value of the operand.	x / y = 4
Modulus	This operator will be	x % y = 0

(%)	dividing the left-hand side value by the right-hand side value of the operand and returns the remainder.	
Exponent (**)	This operator will be doing the 'exponential power' calculation on operands.	x ** y = 16 to the power 4
Floor division (//)	This operator will be dividing the operands, the quotient of a number which is divided by 2 is the result.	13 // 3 = 4, simultaneously 13.0 // 3.0 = 4.0;

Example

Let's see how the output comes. {values in [ ] are outputs}

Let x, y and z be three variables with the following values:

x = 25, y = 30, z = 0:

```
#!/usr/bin/Python3
z = x + y
print(" result of z is ", z)
z = x - y
print("  result of z is ", z)
```

```
z = x * y
print(" result of z is ", z)
z = x / y
print(" result of z is ", z)
z = x % y
print(" result of z is ", z)
```

Output:

```
[z = 35]
[z = -5]
[z = 750]
[z = 0.833]
[z = 5]
```

Now suppose

```
a = 4, b = 5, c = a**b;
print("value of c is", c)
a = 15, b = 45, c = b//a;
print("value of c is", c)
```

Outputs:

```
[value of c is 1024]
```

As 4 to the power 5 is 1024.

```
[value of c is 3]
```

As the quotient of 45/15 is 3.

Python Comparison Operators

In Python, comparison operators are operators that compare two operands' values and returns true or false in case of whether the condition has matched or not. It is also called Python Relational Operator.

Let's take two variables having the values a = 20, b = 15:

Operator	Description	Example
(==)	This condition becomes true only if two given values (operands) are equal.	(a == b) ☐ not true
(!=)	This condition becomes true only if the two operands aren't equal.	(a != b) ☐ true
(>)	This condition becomes true only if the left operand is greater than the right operand.	(a > b) ☐ true
(<)	This condition becomes true only if the right operand is greater than the left operand.	(a < b) ☐ not true
(>=)	This condition becomes true only if the left operand is greater than or equal to the right operator.	(a >= b) ☐ true
(<=)	This condition becomes true only if the right operand is greater than or equal to the left operand.	(a <= b) ☐ not true

Example

Let's see what the output of the following code is:

```
#!/usr/bin/Python3
i = 10
j = 15
if ( i ==j )
      print("i is equal to j")
else
      print("i is not equal to j")
if ( i != i)
      print("i is not equal to j")
else
      print("i is equal to j")
if ( i > j)
      print("i is greater than j")
else
      print("i is not greater than j")
if ( i < j)
    print("i is less than j")
else
    print("i is not less than j")
if ( i >= j)
    print("i is greater than or equal to j")
else
    print("i is neither greater than nor equal to j")
if ( i <= j)
    print ("i is less than or equal to j")
else
    print("i is neither less than nor equal to j")
```

Outputs of the recently used comparison operators:

```
i is not equal to j
i is not equal to j
i is not greater than j
i is less than j
i is neither greater than nor equal to j
i is less than or equal to j
```

Python Assignment Operators

These kinds of operators are used to assign several values to the variables. Let's check the different types of assignment operators.

Operator	Description	Example
Equal (=)	This operator will assign values from right side operand to left side operand.	c = a + b
Add AND (+=)	This operator will add the right operand with left operand and assigns the sum to the left operand.	c += a ☐ it is equivalent to c = c + a;
Subtract AND (-=)	This operator will subtract the right operand from the left operand and assigns the subtraction to the left operand.	c -= a ☐ it is equivalent to c = c - a
Multiply AND (*=)	This operator will multiply the right and left operand and assigns the multiplication to the left operand.	c *= a ☐ it is equivalent to c = c * a
Divide AND	This operator will divide	c /= a

(/=)	the left operand with the right operand and assigns division to the left operand.	□ it's equivalent to c = c/a
Modulus AND (%=)	This operator takes modulus by using both sides' operand and assigns the outcome to left operand.	c %= a □ it's equivalent to c = c % a
Exponent AND (**=)	Does 'to the power' calculation and assigns the outcome to the left operand.	c **= a □ it's equivalent to c = c**a
Floor division AND (//=)	It does floor division and assigns the outcome to the left operand.	c //= a □ it's equivalent to c = c // a

Example

```
#!/usr/bin/Python3
a = 15
b = 20
c = 0
c = a + b
print("value of c is", c)
c += a
print("value of c is", c)
```

```
c *= a
print("value of c is", c)
c %= a
print("value of c is", c)
```

Output: 35, 50, 525, 5 are the outputs of the operators respectively.

Python Bitwise Operators

Bitwise operators are used to perform bit operations. All the decimal values will be converted in the binary format here.

Let's suppose:

a = 0101 1010

b = 0001 1000

Then, it will be

(a & b) = 0001 1000

(a | b) = 0101 1010

(a ^ b) = 0100 0010

(~a) = 1010 0101

Note: There is an in-built function [bin ()] in Python that can obtain the binary representation of an integer number.

Types of Bitwise Operators: [a = 0001 1000, b = 0101 1010]

Operators	Description	Example
Binary AND (&)	This operator executes a bit if it exists in both operands.	(a & b) is 0001 1000
Binary OR (|)	This operator executes a bit if it exists in one of the operands.	(a | b) is 0101 1010
Binary XOR (^)	This operator executes a bit if it is fixed in one operand but not in both	(a ^ b) is 0100 0010
Binary one's complement (~)	This operator executes just by flipping the bits.	~a = 1110 ~b = 0110
Binary left shift (<<)	This operator executes by moving left operand's value more left. It's specified by the right operand.	a << 100 (means 0110 0000)
Binary right shift (>>)	This operator executes by moving left operand's value right. It's specified by the right operand.	a >> 134 (means 0000 0110)

Let's see an example:

```
#!/usr/bin/Python3
a = 50                          # 50 = 0011 0010
b = 17                          # 17 = 0001 0001
print('a=', a, ':', bin(a))
print('b=', b, ':', bin(b))
c = 0
c = a & b;                      # 16 = 0001 0000
print("result of AND is", c, ':', bin(c))
c = a | b;              # 51 = 0011 0011
print("result of OR is", c, ':', bin(c))
c = a ^ b;              # 66 = 0100 0010
print("result of XOR is", c, ':', bin(c))
c = a>> 2;              # 96 = 0110 0000
print("result of right shift is", c, ':', bin(c))
```

Output:

```
a=50: 00110010
b=17: 00010001
result of AND is 16: 0b010000
result of OR is 51: 0b110011
result of XOR is 66: 0b01000010
result of right shift is 96: 0b01100000
```

Python Logical Operator

The logical operator permits a program to make decisions according to multiple conditions. Every operand is assumed as a condition that can give us a true or false value. There are 3 types of logical operators.

(a = false operand, b = true operand)

Operators	Description	Example
Logical AND	If the given operands both are true, the condition becomes true	Condition is false
Logical OR	If one of the given operands is true, the condition becomes true.	Condition is true
Logical NOT	If the given operand is true, the condition becomes false.	Condition is true for a and false for b

Let's see an example:

```
>>> i = 25
# Logical AND Example
>>> if i < 30 AND i > 18:
print (" Condition is fulfilled ")
else:
print(" Condition is not fulfilled ")
```

```
# Logical OR Example
>>> if i < 18 OR i > 20:
print(" Condition is fulfilled ")
else:
print(" Condition is not fulfilled ")
```

Output:

```
Condition is fulfilled
Condition is fulfilled
```

Python Membership Operator

Membership operators are operators that validate the membership of a value. It examines for membership in a sequence like strings, lists, tuples, etc. Two types of membership operators are:

Operator	Description	Example
in	The condition becomes true if it can find a variable in a specified sequence.	Follow the example part given below.
not in	The condition becomes true if it can find no variable in a specified sequence.	Follow the example part given below.

Example

```
#!/usr/bin/Python3
i = 40, j = 20;
listValues = {10, 20, 30, 40}
if( i is in the listValues )
print(" i is available in the list ")
else
print(" i is not available in the list ")
if(j is in the listValues)
print(" j is available in the list ")
```

```
else
print(" j is not available in the list ")
k = i / j
if( k is in the listValues)
print (" k is available in the list ")
else
print(" k is not available in the list ")
```

Output:

```
i is no available in the list
j is not available in the list
k is available in the list
```

Python Identity Operators

These are operators that are used to determine whether a value is of a particular class or type. To determine the type of data that contains several variables, this type of operator is used. There are two types of Identity operators as shown below:

Operator	Description	Example
is	The condition becomes true if the variables of each side of the operator are pointing to the same object.	If id(x) and id(y) are equal and x is y, the result is in 1.
is not	The condition becomes true if the variables of each side of the operator do not point to the same object.	If id(x) and id(y) are not equal and x is not y, the result is not in 1.

Example

```
#!/usr/bin/example3
x = 10, y = 10
print('x = ', 'x', ':', id(x), 'y = ', 'y', ':', id(y)
)
if (x is y)
print(" Both x and y are having same identity ")
```

```
else
print(" x and y are not having same identity ")
if( id(x) == id(y) )
print(" Both x and y are having same identity ")
else
print(" x and y are not having same identity ")
```

Output:

```
x = 10 : 2371593036  y = 10 : 2371593036
Both x and y are having same identity
Both x and y are having same identity
```

Python Operator Precedence

In the below table all the operators from higher to lower precedence are listed

Operator	Description
**	Exponentiation(raise to the power)
~ + -	First one is Complement, second is unary plus and last one is unary minus.
/ * % //	Division, multiplication, modulus, floor division
+ -	Addition and subtraction
>> <<	Right bitwise shift and left bitwise shift
&	Bitwise AND
^ |	Bitwise exclusive OR and bitwise regular OR
<= < > >=	Less than equals to, less than, greater than, greater than equals to (comparison operators)
== <> !=	Equality operators
= %= /= //= -	Assignment Operators

= += *= **=		
is is not	Identity Operators	
In not in	Membership Operators	
NOT OR AND	Logical Operators	

Example

For example, x = 5 + 14 * 2; in this equation, the value of x is 33, not 38 because the operator * has higher precedence than +. For which it first multiplies 14 * 2 and then add it with 5.

Chapter 5:   Data Structures

In this chapter, we are going to explore the different data structures in Python.

Sequence

A sequence is a very basic term in Python that is used to denote the ordered set of values. There are many sequence data types in Python: str, unicode, list, tuple, buffer, and xrange.

Tuples

A tuple consists of some values separated by commas. Tuples are also a sequence data type in Python, like strings and lists. We need to keep in mind that tuples are immutable. It means that they can't be changed.

The tuples consist of the number of values separated by a comma. The tuples are enclosed in parentheses, while the lists are enclosed in brackets.

Now let's see an example:
```
>>> m = (14, 34, 56)
>>> m
(14, 34, 56)
>>> m[0]
```

```
14
>>> m[ 0:2 ]
(14, 34)
```

Tuples also have the properties like indexing and slicing.
Tuples can be nested. Elements in a tuple can be grouped
with ()

Now let's see an example:
```
i = 1
j = 2
t1 = i, j        # is a tuple consists to elements i and
j
t2 = (3, 4, 5)        # is a tuple consists to elements
3,4 and 5
t3 = 0, t1, t2              # is a tuple consists to
elements 0, t1 and t2
print t3        # result is (0, (1, 2), (3, 4, 5))
```

Lists

A list consists of some heterogeneous values separated by
commas enclosed by [and] and started from index 0. Lists can
be used to group other values. Unlike Tuples, Lists are
mutable. In other words, they can be changed by removing or
reassigning existing values. Also, new elements can be
inserted into the existing ones.

Now let's see an example:

```
>>> a = [1, 2, 3, 4, 5]
>>> a
[1, 2, 3, 4, 5]
```

As strings, lists can also be indexed and sliced.

```
>>> a = [1, 2, 3, 4, 5]
>>> a
[1, 2, 3, 4, 5]
>>> a[0]
1
>>> a[4]
5
>>> a[ 0:2 ]
[1, 2]
>>> a[ 3:5 ]
[4, 5]
```

Unlike strings, lists are mutable (i.e. the values can be changed)

```
>>> b = [1, 2, 4, 7, 9]
>>> b
[1, 2, 4, 7, 9]
>>> b[2] = 6
>>> b
[1, 2, 6, 7, 9]  # Here the index [2] is changed to 6
(the initial value is 4)
>>> b[0] = 9
```

```
>>> b
[9, 2, 6, 7, 9]
# Here the index [0] is changed to 9 (the initial value
is 1)
```

The values in the list can be separated by using comma (,)
between the square bracket. Lists can be nested. List can be
used as a Stack or a Queue. For example:

```
list1 = [ 1, 2, 3, 4]
print len (list1) # returns 4 - which is the length of
the list
list1[2] # returns 3 - which is third element in the
list Starts
list1[-1] # returns 4 - which is extreme last element
in the list
list1[-2] # returns 3 - which is extreme last but one
element
list1[ 0:2 ] = [ 11, 22] # replacing first two elements
1 and 2 with 11 and 22
stackList = [ 1, 2, 3, 4]
stackList.append(5) # inserting 5 from the last in the
stack
print stackList # result is: [1, 2, 3, 4, 5]
stackList.pop() #  removing 5 from the stack  Last In
First Out
print stackList # result is: [1, 2, 3, 4]
queueList = [1, 2, 3, 4]
queueList.append(5) # inserting 5 from the last in the
queue
```

```
print queueList # result is: [1, 2, 3, 4, 5]
del(queueList[0] ) #  removing 1 from the queue  First
In First Out
print queueList # result is: [2, 3, 4, 5]
```

Sets

A set doesn't have any duplicate elements present in it and it is an unordered collection type. It means it will have all distinct elements in it with no repetition.

Now let's see an example:

```
fruits = ['apple', 'orange', 'apple', 'pear', 'orange',
'banana']
basket = set (fruits) # removed the duplicate element
apple
print 'orange' in basket # checking orange in basket,
result is True
print 'pineapple' in basket # checking pine apple in
basket, result is False
a = set('aioeueoiaeaeiou') # create a set without
duplicates
b = set('bcokcbzo') # create a set without duplicates
print a # a = ['a', 'i', 'e', 'u', 'o']
print b #   b = ['z', 'c', 'b', 'k', 'o']
print a & b # letters in both a and b  ( A ∩ B )
print a | b # letters in either a or b  ( A ⊠ B )
print a - b # letters in a but not in b ( A - B )
```

Dictionaries

Dictionaries are the data structures in Python that are indexed by keys.

Key and values separated by ":" and pairs of keys separated by a comma and enclosed by { and }

Lists cannot be used as keys.

Now let's see an example:

```
capitals = { 'AP' : 'Hyderabad', 'MH' : 'Mumbai' }
capitals[ 'TN' ] = 'Chennai'
print capitals[ 'AP' ]# returns value of AP in the
dictionary
del capitals[ 'TN' ] # deletes TN from the dictionary
capitals[ 'UP' ] = 'Luck now'  # adding UP to the
dictionary
print 'AP' in capitals    # checks where AP key exist
in dictionary
print 'TN' in capitals
Numbers  = {'1': 'One', '2': 'Two'}
for key, value in Numbers.iteritems() :
     print key, value
```

Strings

In Python, a string is identified by the characters in quotes, such as single (") and double (""). They can only store character values and are primitive datatype. Please note that strings are altogether different from integers or numbers. Therefore, if you declare a string "111", then it has no relation with the number 111.

```
>>> print "hello"
hello
>>> print 'good'
good
```

The string index starts from 0 in Python.

```
>>> word = 'hello'
>>> word[0]
'h'
>>> word[2]
'l'
```

Indices may also be negative numbers, to start counting from the right. Please note that negative indices start from -1 while positive indices start from 0 (since -0 is same as 0).

```
>>> word = 'good'
>>> word[-1]
'd'
>>> word[-2]
'o'
```

The slicing in Python is used to obtain substrings, while index allows us to obtain a single character.

```
>>> word = 'develop'
>>> word[ 0:2 ]
```

```
'de'
>>> word[ 2:4 ]
've'
```

Please note that the starting position is always included and the ending position is always excluded.

```
D e v e l o p
0 1 2 3 4 5 6 ---- Index value
```

In the above example, the word is assigned a value develop. Considering the first statement word [0:2], the output is 'de'. Here the starting position 'd' (0th index) is included and the ending position 'v' (2nd index) is excluded. Similarly, in the second statement word [2:4], the starting position 'v' (2nd index) is included and the ending position 'l' (4th index) is excluded.

The important point to be noted is that Python strings are immutable (i.e. Strings cannot be changed).

There are many in-built functions available with a String. They are used for various purposes. Let's see some of the basic ones that are most commonly used.

Len: It is the length function that is used to calculate the number of characters present in the string.

Lower: It will convert all the uppercase characters present in the string to lowercase letters. Therefore, after using this function, all characters in the string will be small case only.

Upper: It will convert all the lowercase characters present in the string to uppercase letters. Therefore, after using this function, all characters in the string will be upper case only.

Split: It helps to split the string into parts by using a delimiter. It can be separated using spaces, new lines, commas, or tabs.

Control Flow Statements

If–else statement

The if-else statement is used to make the choices from 2 or more statements. It becomes helpful when you want to execute a particular statement based on a True or False condition.

The syntax of if statement is:

If condition:

   action-1   # Indentation

Else:

action-2   # Indentation

Here the indentation is required. The actions action-1 and action-2 may consist of many statements but they must be all indented.

if <expression> :

<statements>

else :

<statements>

The example is shown below.

```
>>> e = 6
>>> f = 7
>>> if(e < f):
...     print( 'f is greater than e' )
... else:
...     print(' e is greater than f')
...
```

Output: f is greater than e

```
def  numberProperty1 ( input ) :
        if input % 2 ==  0 :
print input , ' is an Even number '
        else :
print input , ' is an Odd number '
numberProperty1( 10 )    # result is 10 is an Even
```

```
number
numberProperty1( 11 )     # result is 11 is an Odd
number
```

Nested If

It consists of more than 2 statements to choose from.

```
def numberProperty2 ( input ) :
if input < 0:
print input , ' is a Negative number '
elif input == 0:
print input , ' is Zero '
else:
print input , ' is a Positive number '
numberProperty2( -100 )  # -100  is a Negative number
numberProperty2( 0 )        # 0  is Zero
numberProperty2( 100 )   # 100  is a Positive number
```

While Loop

The while loop will run until the expression is true and it stops once it is false.

The syntax of while loop is:

While expression:

 statement

For example:

```
>>> a = 1
>>> while(a < 10 ):
...     print "The number is:" , a
...     a = a + 1
...
The number is: 1
The number is: 2
The number is: 3
The number is: 4
The number is: 5
The number is: 6
The number is: 7
The number is: 8
The number is: 9
The number is: 10
```

In the above example, the block consists of print and increment statements, it is executed repeatedly until the count is no longer less than 5.

In the following example the while loop is implemented within a function:

```
def printSeries( start, end, interval ) :
print " \n "
temp = start
while ( temp < end ) :
print temp,
temp += interval
printSeries( 1, 11, 1 )    # result is  1 2 3 4 5 6 7 8
```

```
 9 10
printSeries( 1, 11, 3 )    # result is  1 4 7 10
```

For Statement

Any object with an iteration method can be used in a for loop in Python. The iteration method means that the data can be presented in a list form where there are multiple values in an ordered manner. The syntax of for loop is:

for item in list:

  action   # Indentation

The action consists of one or more statements and it must be indented. The examples are shown below.

For example:

```
>>> for i in (1, 2, 3, 4, 5, 6, 7, 8, 9, 10):
...      print i
...
1
2
3
4
5
6
7
8
9
```

```
10
>>> list = ['a', 'bb', 'ccc', 'dddd']
>>> for l in list:
...       print l,len(l)
...
a 1
bb 2
ccc 3
dddd 4
```

The above program shows that the values of a list and its length are printed using the for loop.

Functions

A function is a block of organized and reusable code that is used to perform related tasks. We can break our huge lines of programming code into smaller modules with the help of functions. It also helps in avoiding repetitions of code, as we don't need to write the same lines of code again and again. Instead, we can write it once inside a function and then use the function anywhere in the program.

You need to make sure that the function name is unique.

Rules to define a function in Python

In Python, a function is defined using the keyword def. The arguments will be placed within the parenthesis ().

Now let's see an example:

```
>>> def printdetails(name, age):
...         print "Name:", name;
...         print "Age:", age;
...         return;
...
>>> printdetails(name = "Mary", age = 30);
Name: Mary
Age: 30
```

In the above example 'printdetails' is the function name and 'name' and 'age' are the parameters.

Syntax of user defined method

def < function name> :

[< declaration of local variables >]

[< statements >]

Now let's see an example:

```
Language = "Python"
def printString( input ) :
print input
def multiply ( x, y ) :
return x * y
def power( x, y):
return x ** y
printString( Language )        # returns Python
```

```
z = multiply( 10, 20 )
print z# returns 200 - which is equal to 10 * 20
print power( 10, 2 )   # returns 100 - which is equal
to 10 ** 2
```

Accepting inputs during the runtime

raw_input() is a built-in Python function that provides the facility to accept input during the execution of the script

Now let's see an example:

```
name = raw_input( "\n Please enter your name : " )
```

This statement provides a message to the user to provide input for a name.

Control Statements

Break

The break statement breaks out of the smallest enclosing for or while loop.

Now let's see an example:

```
def primeNumberValidation ( input ) :
        for x in range( 2, input ) :
                if  input % x == 0:
        print  input, 'is not a prime number and equals',
    x, '*',  input/x
        break
```

```
    else:
        print  input, 'is a prime number'
    primeNumberValidation( 3 )
    primeNumberValidation( 14 )
```

Continue

The continue statement continues with the next iteration of the loop.

Now let's see an example:

```
def evenNumbers( start, end ) :
print "\n\nEven numbers in between ", start , " and ",
end
for n in range( start + 1, end ) :
if n % 2 != 0:
continue
print n
evenNumbers( 1, 11 )   # result is  14 is 2 4 6 8 10
evenNumbers( 10, 30 ) # result is  12 14 16 18 20 22 24
26 28
```

Pass

The pass is a valid statement and can be used when there is a statement required syntactically, but the program requires no action.

Now let's see an example:

```
while True :
        pass  # In condition loop press (Ctrl + c) for
the keyboard interrupt
```

In this example, while followed by "pass" it does not execute any statement.

There is a necessity to include at least one statement in a block (e.g. function, while, for loop, etc.) in these cases, use pass as one statement, which does nothing but includes one statement under ':'

Now let's see an example:
```
def  x() :
pass  # one valid statement that does not do any
action
```

Here pass is considered a statement for the declaration of function x.

String Manipulation

We can use built-in functions to manipulate strings in Python. The package "string" provides more functions on strings.

For example:
```
print name = "ABCD XYZ xyz"
print len(name) # It will return the length of the
```

```
string name
print list(name) # It will return the list of
characters in name print
name.startswith( 'A' ) # It will return True if name
starts with A else returns False
print name.endswith( 'Z' ) # It will return True if
name ends with Z else returns False
print name.index( 'CD' ) # It will return the index of
CD in name
print 'C'.isalpha( ) # It will return True if C is
alpha or returns False
print '1'.isdigit( ) # It will return True if 1 is
digit or returns False
print name.lower( ) # It will return a string with
lowercase characters in name
print name.upper( ) # It will return a string with
uppercase characters in name
```

Exception Handling

Exceptions are the errors detected during execution and these are not unconditionally fatal.

Exception blocks will be enclosed with try and except statements.

try :

<statements>

except <exception type > :

<statements>

Let's see an example:

```
# Defining an exception block
try:
    print ( 1 / 0 )
except Exception as excep:
    print "exception : ", excep
# Defining a user-defined exception
class UserDefinedException( Exception ) :
    def __init__(self, value):
        self.value = value
    def __str__(self):
        return repr(self.value)
# Raising a user-defined exception explicitly
try:
    raise UserDefinedException(" input is null ")
except UserDefinedException as userdefinedexception:
    print 'userdefinedexception :
', userdefinedexception.value
```

In the above-mentioned program, first (try, except, block) handles the Zero division exception.

UserDefinedException is a user-defined exception to raise business exceptions in the program.

Second (try, except) block raises a user-defined exception.

Chapter 6:   Learning about Functions

So far, we have learned quite a lot of things. If you have already started to lose track of all the knowledge, you shouldn't be alarmed. It is only natural for everyone to find themselves in such a situation when they are in the learning process. No one is perfect and that is what makes us all human beings, right?

We have seen dictionaries and learned they are nothing like the ones we use to learn new words and meanings. We have learned about a rather funny thing called tuples and understood that they are essentially a list with parentheses and do not allow anyone to add, remove, or modify values. We have gone initially through some functions too, but now it is time for us to start looking into functions a little more closely.

Understanding the Concept of Function

Take a moment or two here and engage your mind a little. Think about it and try to come up with some vague idea of what functions truly are.

Functions are either user-defined or pre-defined. In either case, their job is to organize codes within a recallable function name. There are tons of pre-defined functions available within Python. We have already been using some of these again and again.

We already have a decent idea about functions that are built-in and pre-defined. These include and are not limited to input(), print(), and so many more. However, let's now look at how to create our function.

Let's begin with a traditional approach and write a block of code that welcomes the user with a friendly greeting. We will store this as a function named "welcome_message" so that we can call on this function later on.

```python
def welcome_message():
    print("Hello and welcome")
    print("Hope you have a great time")
print("Begin")
welcome_message()
print("End")
```

Let's begin learning and see what is happening in the block of code above. Firstly, for us to create our function, we need to define it first. The 'def' is a keyword that Python will look at and immediately understand that you are about to 'define' a new function. Next, we will need to name the function. While you can always name the function as you please, it is highly recommended and encouraged that you use names that are easy to understand and have a descriptive name. If we were to name this function anything other than welcome_message, we may know what it is as we wrote it, but for any other programmer out there, they may not understand.

Whenever you create a function, you need to use parentheses. You do not have to pass any information through it so leave them as they are. Now, we need to add the colon mark.

What happens when you use a colon at the end of a statement? Your cursor gets indented in the following line. That means your cursor will be slightly far from the actual starting point. This is to denote to the programmer that he/she is about to type something that would hold value for a command or a statement above it. In this case, we are trying to define the function.

Let's then use two print commands and place our greeting messages. That is it! You have now created your very first function. You can now recall it as many times as you like. However, should you try to call on this function a line or two before the 'def' command, Python will have no idea what you're talking about. Why? That has everything to do with the fact that Python reads a program line by line. By the time it arrives on the line where you called a function, it would check with the previous lines and not find anything relatable as the actual 'def' step was carried out in a step following this.

After this, let's now use our function and see how it works. Remember, the function holds two printable messages for our users. For our reference, we will now create a 'begin' and an 'end' message. This would allow us and the programmer to know where the regular messages are and where the function lies. Use your function with empty parentheses between the two print commands as shown above. If you like, you can remove these print commands and just type in your function number to see the results.

A quick tip for all! If you come across the annoying wiggly lines, simply hover your mouse over them and you will find out what the expected or suggested solution is. In this case, if you remove the two-line spaces, you should see a suggestion saying this:

```
PycharmProjects\My 1    def welcome_message():
               2        print("Hello and welcome")
               3        print("Hope you have a great time")
               4    print("Begin")
```

PEP 8: expected 2 blank lines after class or function definition, found 0

Reformat file Alt+Shift+Enter   More actions... Alt+Enter

Whenever you define a function, you will always be required

to leave at least two blank lines before proceeding on with the codes.

Now, let's run the program and you should see all the messages and our function in action. Python initiated the sequence and first read the definition. This is where Python only understood for itself what the function was. The actual program was executed when Python reached line six, where our print("Begin") message started. In the next line, we placed our function and this is where Python recalled what it had just learned. It quickly carried out the set of codes we defined within the function and executed the same. Lastly, it executed the last line before finishing the program.

This is how functions are created and used. Now, we can use this function as many times as we like within the same file. Note that you cannot use this newly created function if you were to open a new file or work on an older file where you did not define this function.

When things start to get tougher for you in your programming future, remember to create your functions and use them where applicable. They will save you quite a lot of time and help you in places as well. These are used when certain actions or operations need to be carried out every now and then.

Using Various Functions

Python was created with simplicity in mind. It was also created to minimize the work and maximize the output. If you use the codes and the functions wisely, you will surely be making the most out of this programming language. It is also noticeable that most of the things you learn about Python and its functions, parameters, methods, and such will help you learn other languages quicker, so do pay attention.

Parameters

Our eagle-eyed readers may have noticed something about the function we just created a few minutes ago. Unlike most of the functions, we did not pass any information through the parentheses at all. Why that happens is something we will come to know about once we understand exactly what parameters are in Python.

Parameters are used as place-holders for receiving information. These are what we, as well as users, provide to the program in order for it to work more accurately. There are some cases and functions where arguments are not required for them to do their basic operation. However, if you provide an argument to these functions, they will provide you with a more specific output. Of course, it does depend on the availability of the said parameter. You cannot force a function to do something it is not designed to do.

Now, let's look at our function. It is certainly missing something. If you currently print the welcome_user function, it would say everything but will not contain the name of the user at all. Surely, it would look a lot nicer for us if we could somehow use this function to use the name of the user and add it to the greeting.

Luckily, we can do just that! For that, we first need to add the 'name' parameter in the first line, where we began defining our function. Simple type name between the parentheses and you will see the text turn grey. This confirms that the word has been added as a parameter. Now, we wish to print the name of this user along with the greetings we have defined within the function. For this example, let's assume that the user is named Fred.

```
def welcome_message(name):
    print("Begin")
    print("Hello and welcome {name}!")
    print("Hope you have a great time")
    print("End")
welcome_message('Fred')
Begin
Hello and welcome Fred!
Hope you have a great time
End
```

Finally! We have a name to add to our greetings. You can add another line of code by using our function and passing a different name now. See what happens then.

When we set a parameter for a function and then call upon the function without providing it with an argument or the bit of information that goes between the parentheses, it will provide us with an error, except for a few.

Now, let's make our function a little more dynamic and add another parameter. Let's add a parameter that allows the program to print out the last name of the user. Now, our code should look something like this:

```python
def welcome_message(name, last_name):
    print("Hello and welcome {name} {last_name}!")
    print("Hope you have a great time")
print("Begin")
welcome_message('Fred', 'William')
print("End")
```

The point to learn here, apart from being able to add parameters, is the fact that 'Fred' and 'William' are being used in a specific order. Should you type it the other way around, Python will print these as they are. This is because of their position concerning the defined parameters. The first value Python reads here, it will automatically link it with the first parameter. This can cause a little confusion, especially if the last name becomes the first name.

These arguments are called as positional arguments. To further show their importance, let's remove the last name from the argument above.

```
print("Begin")
welcome_message('Fred')
print("End")
Traceback (most recent call last):
Begin
  File
"C:/Users/Smith/PycharmProjects/MyFirstGo/PosArg.py",
line 7, in <module>
    welcome_message('Fred')
TypeError: welcome_message() missing 1 required
positional argument: 'last_name'
```

So, the system does not allow us to continue as we have removed an element. This time, type in the last name first followed by the first name and see if it makes any difference. When you run the program now, you should be able to see this:

```
print("Begin")
welcome_message('Fred', 'William')
print("End")
Begin
Hello and welcome William Fred!
Hope you have a great time
End
```

Now, the sequence kind of worked. The only issue is that it has gotten the name wrong. Now, the last name is being portrayed and printed as the first name. That is rather embarrassing, isn't it?

The above errors either state that we are missing one required positional argument or show that we placed the wrong name in the wrong place. Positional arguments are such arguments whose position matters a lot. If you miss out on the position altogether, you will end up with an error. If you type in something else, as we did in our last example, you will produce incorrect results. To correct it, simply provide the last name after the first name.

There is one more way you can have these dealt with by using what is termed as 'keyword arguments'. These are the kind of arguments whose position does not matter at all and Python will still continue to function properly regardless of their position in the parentheses. To pass a keyword argument, you will need to do the following:

```
print("Begin")
welcome_message(last_name='William', name='Fred')
print("End")
Begin
Hello and welcome Fred William!
Hope you have a great time
End
```

Now that's more like it. Things are looking right at how we want them. Notice how, even though we wrote in the wrong order, Python picked up and sorted the order for us. That is because we made our entries or arguments into keyword arguments using the name= or last_name= parameter and combining it with arguments. This allows Python to draw information and understand which of these two comes first in order as defined originally in our function.

Factually speaking, you will not be using these quite a lot, but it is always an advantage to know the ways to overcome certain issues. Normally, you or any other programmer would be able to see the data and read it easily if you simply follow the rules and type the first name followed by the last name. Make the code as easy as you can for everyone to read and understand.

"Well, what if I was using numbers instead of names?"

That is one fine question. This is where you will need to use keyword arguments to represent what those values are for. You might be running a function that involves multiple values that only you might be able to understand, but others will have no idea where they came from. You must label each one of them with the relevant keyword argument so that the readability increases.

We are currently just beginning and for the sake of demonstration, we used a simple example to showcase how to create functions and use them. Your functions, when the time comes, might be quite vast or equally short, depending on the kind of function you create in any specific situation.

Creating functions certainly helps us organize our codes and be more efficient and effective. If we were unable to do this, we would have had to resort to writing the same bunch of lines every now and then.

Return Statement

We could have covered what a return statement is when we were discussing 'if' statements and others. However, it makes more sense to learn this after you have understood the concept of parameters and functions.

So far, we have created a function that has allowed us to send information via the use of parameters. However, when we talk about return statements, these are designed to do certain calculations and provide us with the results instead of us feeding it with values.

Let's look a little deeper into how this works by creating our second function. The purpose of this function is based on a simple math trick which most of us might have heard of or played with when we were young. Ask the user to think of any number and you would ask them to add and subtract a few simple numbers. Eventually, you would provide them with an accurate result and everyone would be shocked. Now, let's reveal what happens with the use of this function we are about to create.

```python
def magic_number(number):
    return number + 6 - 4 + 5 - number
```

This simple calculation would always return you the value of seven. Go ahead, try it out yourself by doing this. However, for us to be able to get these values back, we have used the return statement here. This tells Python that it is supposed to do the calculation for us and then only return the resulting value instead of printing each of these individually.

Let's give our second function a test run:

```python
result = magic_number(8329)
print(result)
```

See how the result now shows as seven? You can try and change the values to whatever you please, the result will continue to remain as seven. That is only made possible owing to the return statement we have provided here. If you take away the keyword return, you end up with a value that says 'None'. The program will still function, but the result would no longer be calculated or of any use to us. This is because Python would not execute a return phase and thus will not carry out the calculations as we would like it to.

Using these can greatly enhance your experience as a programmer or a user. However, before you dive in and start creating your functions, here are some which are pre-defined and may come in handy. There is no point in creating a function and finding out Python already had one for you.

1. min() and max() - In case you run into various values and you quickly wish to find out the minimum value in existence within a list or collection of data, use the min() command and run the numbers through. The minimum number will be printed for you. The max() function is the opposite, of course!

2. sum() - This is quite a nifty function and allows you to quickly add up all the numbers in the list and produce the result for you right away. The accuracy with floats might not be what we like, but hey, it gets you going.

3. type() - There may come lines and lines of codes with variables that are scattered all over the place. You now wish to find out where the variable started from and what kind of a variable it is. Using the type() function, you can quickly find out what kind of variable you are dealing with. It will return values such as 'bool' to indicate that the variable in question is a bool in type.

There are hundreds of functions that you will start to learn as you proceed into advanced Python learning and machine learning. However, to understand most of them, you will need to practice these and develop a thorough understanding of how this works. You should then have no problems venturing into a more advanced version of Python learning and developing complex programs.

Test your knowledge

This time, let's raise the stakes a bit and test your knowledge. This will involve a combination of everything you have learned so far. However, this time you will not be provided with solutions to keep you on a quest to search for answers and use a bit of trial and error method to perfect the program.

Exercise

Here is the updated version of a program we designed to check insurance prices a person would have to pay if he/she was above or below a certain age. Your objective is to convert this into a function. Your function should have three fields set to receive input from the user.

- Name
- Age
- Actual insurance cost

Updated code:

```
Insurance = 1000
age = int(input('Your age: '))
is_old = age > 40
is_young = age <= 28
has_license = input('Do you have a license? ')
if has_license.lower() == 'Yes':
    has_license = True
elif has_license.lower() != 'Yes':
    has_license = False
if is_old and has_license:
    Insurance = Insurance / 2
    print("Your insurance cost is ${Insurance}")
elif is_young and has_license:
    Insurance = Insurance // 1.50
    print("You will need to pay ${Insurance}")
else:
    print('You are not eligible for insurance at this
time')
```

Chapter 7:   Conditional and Loops in Python

This chapter describes moderate level topics like conditionals and loops in detail. We will use different examples to explain these topics in detail. Let's dive into knowing more about these concepts.

What is a sequence in Python?

The sequence of program execution is not a highway linking the north and the south. It can run from the north to the south to the end. The sequence of program execution may be as complicated as a highway in a busy area, with nine turns and 18 turns, which is easy to make people dizzy.

To write a good program, it is very important to control the process of program execution. Therefore, it is necessary to use the process control structure of the program. Without them, it is impossible to use the program to complete any complicated work.

The programming language has been continuously developed for decades. Structured Programming has gradually become the mainstream of program development. Its main idea is to execute the entire program in sequence from top to bottom. Python language is mainly executed from top to bottom according to the sequence of program source code, but sometimes the execution sequence will be changed according to needs.

At this time, the computer can be told which sequence to execute the program preferentially through flow control instructions. The process control of the program is like designing a traffic direction extending in all directions for the highway system.

It is recognized that most program codes for process control are executed in sequence from top to bottom line after line, but for operations with high repeatability, it is not suitable to execute in sequence. Any Python program, no matter how complex its structure is, can be expressed or described using three basic control processes: sequence structure, selection structure, and loop structure.

The first line statement of the sequence structure program is the entry point and is executed from top to bottom to the last line statement of the program. The selection structure allows the program to select the program block to be executed according to whether the test condition is established or not. If the condition is True, some program statements are executed. If the condition is False, other program statements are executed.

Colloquially, if you encounter a situation A, perform operation A; if this is case b, operation b is executed. Just like when we drive to the intersection and see the signal lamp, the red light will stop, and the green light will pass. Also, different destinations also have different directions, and you can choose the route according to different situations. In other words, the selection structure represents that the program will determine the "direction" of the program according to the specified conditions.

The function of loop flow control with loop structure is to repeatedly execute the program statements in a program block until the specific ending conditions are met. Python has a for loop and a while loop.

Selection Process Control

Selection Process Control is a conditional control statement that contains a conditional judgment expression (also referred to as conditional expression or conditional judgment expression for short). If the result of the conditional judgment expression is True (true), a program block is executed. If the result of the conditional judgment expression is false (True), another program block is executed.

The following describes the statements and their functions related to the selection process control in Python language.

If...Else Conditional Statement

If...else conditional statement is a fairly common and practical statement. If the conditional judgment expression is True (true, or represented by 1), the program statement in the if program block is executed. If the conditional judgment expression is not true (False, or represented by 0), the program statement in the else program block is executed. If there are multiple judgments, elif instruction can be added.

The syntax of the if conditional statement is as follows:

If the conditional judgment expression holds, execute the program statement in this program block

Else :

If the condition does not hold, execute the program statement in this program block. If we want to judge whether the value of variable a is greater than or equal to the value of variable b, the condition judgment expression can be written as follows:

If a >= b:

\# If A is greater than or equal to B, execute the program statement in this program block

Else :

\# If a is NOT greater than or equal to b, the program statement if ... if...else conditional statement in this program block is executed.

In the use of the if...else conditional statement, if the condition is not satisfied, there is no need to execute any program statement, and the else part can be omitted

If conditional judgment expression

\# If the condition is satisfied, execute the program statements in this program block. Besides, if the if...else conditional statement uses logical operators such as "and", it is suggested to add parentheses to distinguish the execution order to improve the readability of the program,

For example: if (a==c) and (a>b):

\# If A equals C and A is greater than B, execute the program statement in this program block

Else :

If the above condition does not hold, the program statement in this program block is executed.

Also, Python language provides a more concise conditional expression of if...else in the following format: X if C else Y returns one of the two expressions according to the conditional judgment expression. In the above expression, X is returned when C is true; otherwise, Y is returned.

For example, to determine whether the integer x is odd or even, the original program would be written as follows:

```
If (first % 2)==0:
second= "even number"
Else:
second= "odd number"
```

If print('{0}'.format(second)) is changed to a concise form, only a single line of program statements is required to achieve the same purpose.

The statements are as follows:

```
print('{0}'.format ("even" if (first% 2)==0 else
"odd"))
```

If the if condition determines that the expression is true, it returns "even"; otherwise, it returns "odd." In the following sample program, we will practice the use of the if...else statement. The purpose of the sample program is to make a simple leap year judgment program.

Let the user enter the year (4-digit integer year), and the program will determine whether it is a leap year. One of the following two conditions is a leap year:

1. leap every 4 years (divisible by 4) but not every 100 years (divisible by 100).
2. leap every 400 years (divisible by 400).

[example procedure: leapYear.py]

Determine whether an input year is a leap year or not

```
01 # -*- coding: utf-8 -*-
02 """
03 program name: leap year judging program
04 Topic Requirements:
05 Enter the year (4-digit integer year) to determine
whether it is a leap year
06 condition 1. Every 4 leap (divisible by 4) and every
100 leap (divisible by 100)
07 condition 2. Every 400 leap (divisible by 400)
08 One of the two conditions met is a leap year.
09 """
10 year = int(input ("Give year:"))
12 if (year % 4 == 0 and year % 100 ! = 0) or (year %
400 == 0):
13 print("{0} is a leap year ."format(year))
14 Else:
```

The execution results of the

```
15 print("{0} is the year of peace ."format(year))
```

Program Code Resolution:

Line 10: Enter a year, but remember to call the int () function to convert it to an integer type.

Line 12-15: Judge whether it is a leap year.

Condition 1: every 4 leaps (divisible by 4) and every 100 leaps (not divisible by 100).

Condition 2: every 400 leaps (divisible by 400). One of the two conditions is a leap year. Readers are asked to inquire whether the following years are leap years: 1900 (flat year), 1996 (leap year), 2004 (leap year), 2017 (flat year), 2400 (leap year).

Multiple Choices

If there is more than one conditional judgment expression, elif conditional statement can be added. Elif is like the abbreviation of "else if." Although using multiple if conditional statements can solve the problem of executing different program blocks under various conditions, it is still not simple enough. Then, elif conditional statements can be used, and the readability of the program can be improved.

Note that if the statement is a logical "necessity" in our program. Elif and else do not necessarily follow, so there are three situations: if, if/else, if/elif/else.

The format is as follows:

If condition judgment

Expression 1:

If the conditional judgment expression 1 holds, the program statement in this program block is executed

Elif condition judgment

Expression 2:

If the conditional judgment expression 2 holds, execute the program statement in this program block

Else :

If none of the above conditions hold, execute the program statement in this program block,

For example:

If first==second:

If first equals second, execute the program statement in this

program block

Elif first>second :

If first is greater than second, execute the program statement in this program block

Else :

if first is not equal to second and first is less than second, execute the program statement in this program block.

The following example program is used to practice the use of IF multiple selection. The purpose of the sample program is to detect the current time to decide which greeting to use.

[sample procedure: currentTime.py]

Detects the current time to decide which greeting

```
01 # -*- coding: utf-8 -*-
02 """
03 Program Name: Detect the current time to decide
which greeting to use
04 Topic Requirements:
05 Judging from the current time (24-hour system)
06 5~10:59, output "good morning"
07 11~17:59, output "good afternoon"
08 18~4:59, output "good night"
09 """
```

```
11 import time
13 print ("current time: {}." format (time.strftime
("%h:% m:% s"))
14 h = int( time.strftime("%H") )
16 if h>5 and h < 11:
17 print ("good morning!" )
18 elif h >= 11 and h<18:
19 print ("good afternoon!" )
20 else:
21 print ("good night!")
```

The execution results of the program will be shown on the screen.

The output shows the current time in the sample program to judge whether it is morning, afternoon, or evening, and then displays the appropriate greeting. Python's time module provides various functions related to time. The Time module is a module in Python's standard module library.

Before using it, you need to use the import instruction to import and then call the strftime function to format the time into the format we want. For example, the following program statement is used to obtain the current time.

```
import time
Time.strftime ("%h:% m:% s")
 # 18: 36: 16 (6:36:16 p.m.  24-hour)
Time. strftime ("%i:% m:% s")
# 06:36:16 (6: 36: 16 p.m. 12-hour system) format
```

parameters to be set are enclosed in parentheses.

Pay attention to the case of format symbols. The following program statement is used to display the week, month, day, hour, minute, and second.

Print (time.strftime ("%a,% b% d% h:% m:% s")) execution results are as follows: Monday, sep17 15: 49: 29 4.2.3 nested if sometimes there is another layer of if conditional statement in the if conditional statement. This multi-layer selection structure is called nested if conditional statement.

Usually, when demonstrating the use of nested if conditional statements, it is more common to demonstrate multiple choices with numerical ranges or scores. In other words, different grades of certificates will be issued for different grades of achievements.

If it is more than 60 points, the first certificate of competency will be given, if it is more than 70 points, the second certificate of competency will be given, if it is more than 80 points, the third certificate of competency will be given, if it is more than 90 points, the fourth certificate of competency will be given, if it is more than 100 points, the all-round professional certificate of competency will be given.

Based on nested if statements, we can write the following program:

```
available= int(input ("Give a score:")
if available >= 60:
print ('First Certificate of Conformity')
if available >= 70:
print ('Second Certificate of Conformity')
if available >= 80:
print ('Third Certificate of Conformity')
if available >= 90:
print ('Fourth Certificate of Conformity')
if getScore == 100:
```

Print ('All-round Professional Qualification Certificate') is actually an if statement that is explored layer by layer. We can use the if/elif statement to filter the multiple choices one by one according to conditional expression operation and select the matching condition (True) to execute the program statement in a program block.

The syntax is as follows:

If Conditional Expression 1:

The program block to be executed under conditional expression 1

Elif conditional expression 2:

The program block to be executed under conditional expression 2

Elif conditional expression n:

The program block to be executed according to the conditional expression n

Else:

If all the conditional expressions do not conform, this program block is executed. When the conditional expression 1 does not conform, the program block searches down to the finally conforming conditional expression.

The elif instruction is an abbreviation of else if. Elif statement can generate multiple statements according to the operation of a conditional expression, and its conditional expression must be followed by a colon, which indicates that the following program blocks meet this conditional expression and need to be indented.

The following example program is a typical example of the combined use of nested if and if/elif statements. This program uses if to determine which grade the query results belong to. Also, another judgment has been added to the sample program. If the score integer value entered is not between 0 and 100, a prompt message of "input error, the number entered must be between 0 and 100" will be output.

Comprehensive use of nested if statements example:

```
01 # -*- coding: utf-8 -*-
02 """
03 Examples of Comprehensive Use of Nested if
Statements
04 """
05 result = int(input ('Give final grade:')
06
07 # First Level if/else Statement: Judge whether the
result entered is between 0 and 100
08 if result >= 0 and result <= 100:
09 # 2nd level if/elif/else statement
10 if result <60:
11 print('{0} below cannot obtain certificate of
competency'. format(result))
12 elif result >= 60 and result <70:
13 print('{0} result is d'. format(result))
14 elif result >- 70 and result <80:
15 print('{0} result is c'. format(result))
16 elif result >= 80 and result <90:
17 print('{0} result is level b'. format(result))
18 else:
19 print('{0} result is grade a'. format(result))
20 else:
21 print ('input error, input number must be between 0-
100')
```

Program code analysis:

Lines 7-21: first-level if/else statement, used to judge whether the input result is between 0 and 100.

Lines 10-19: the second-level if/elif/else statement, which is used to judge which grade the inquired result belongs to.

In the next section, we will discuss loops one of the most important concepts.

The Loop Repeat Structure

This mainly refers to the loop control structure. A certain program statement is repeatedly executed according to the set conditions, and the loop will not jump out until the condition judgment is not established. In short, repetitive structures are used to design program blocks that need to be executed repeatedly, that is, to make program code conform to the spirit of structured design.

For example, if you want the computer to calculate the value of 1+2+3+4+...+10, you don't need us to accumulate from 1 to 10 in the program code, which is originally tedious and repetitive, and you can easily achieve the goal by using the loop control structure. Python contains a while loop and a for loop, and the related usage is described below.

While loop

If the number of loops to be executed is determined, then using the for loop statement is the best choice. However, the while loop is more suitable for certain cycles that cannot be determined. The while loop statement is similar to the for loop statement and belongs to the pre-test loop. The working model of the pre-test loop is that the loop condition judgment expression must be checked at the beginning of the loop program block.

When the judgment expression result is true, the program statements in the loop block will be executed. We usually call the program statements in the loop block the "loop body." While loop also uses a conditional expression to judge whether it is true or false to control the loop flow. When the conditional expression is true, the program statement in the loop will be executed. When the conditional expression is false, the program flow will jump out of the loop.

The format of the While loop statement is as follows:

While conditional expression:

If the conditional expression holds, the flow chart of executing the while loop statement in this program block.

The while loop must include the initial value of the control variable and the expression for increasing or decreasing. When writing the loop program, it must check whether the condition for leaving the loop exists. If the condition does not exist, the loop body will be continuously executed without stopping, resulting in an "infinite loop," also called "dead loop."

The loop structure usually requires three conditions:

(1)   The initial value of the loop variable.

(2)   Cyclic conditional expression.

(3)   Adjust the increase or decrease the value of cyclic variables.

For example, the following procedure:

```
first=1
While first < 10: # Loop Condition Expression
print( first)
first += 1 # adjusts the increase or decrease value of
the loop variable.
```

When first is less than 10, the program statement in the while loop will be executed, and then first will be added with 1 until first is equal to 10. If the result of the conditional expression is False, it will jump out of the loop.

For loop

For loop, also known as count loop, is a loop form commonly

used in programming. It can repeatedly execute a fixed number of loops. If the number of loop executions required is known to be fixed when designing the program, then the for-loop statement is the best choice. The for loop in Python language can be used to traverse elements or table items of any sequence. The sequence can be tuples, lists or strings, which are executed in sequence.

The syntax is as follows:

For element variable in sequence:

Executed instructions

The program block of #else can be added or not added, that is, when using the for loop, the else statement can be added or not added. The meaning represented by the above Python syntax is that the for loop traverses all elements in a sequence, such as a string or a list, in the order of the elements in the current sequence (item, or table item).

For example, the following variable values can all be used as traversal sequence elements of a for loop.

```
first= "abcdefghijklmnopqrstuvwxyz "
second= ['january', 'march', 'may', 'july', 'august',
'october', 'december']
result= [a, e, 3, 4, 5, j, 7, 8, 9, 10]
```

Besides, if you want to calculate the number of times a loop is executed, you must set the initial value of the loop, the ending condition, and the increase or decrease value of the loop variable for each loop executed in the for-loop control statement. For loop every round, if the increase or decrease value is not specifically specified, it will automatically accumulate 1 until the condition is met.

For example, the following statement is a tuple (11 ~ 15) and uses the for loop to print out the numeric elements in the tuple: x = [11, 12, 13, 14, 15]

```
for first in x:
    print(first)
```

A more efficient way to write tuples is to call the range () function directly. The format of the range () function is as follows:

range ([initial value], final value [,increase or decrease value])

Tuples start from "initial value" to the previous number of "final value." If no initial value is specified, the default value is 0; if no increase or decrease value is specified, the default increment is 1.

An example of calling the range () function is as follows: range (3) means that starting from the subscript value of 0, 3 elements are output, i.e., 0, 1 and 2 are three elements in total.

Range(1,6) means starting from subscript value 1 and ending before subscript value 6-1, that is, subscript number 6 is not included, i.e., 1, 2, 3, 4 and 5 are five elements. ·range (4,10,2) means starting from subscript value 4 and ending before subscript number 10, that is, subscript number 10 is excluded, and the increment value is 2, i.e., 4, 6 and 8 are three elements. The following program code demonstrates the use of the range () function in a for loop to output even numbers between 2 and 11 for i in range (2, 11, 2).

One more thing to pay special attention to when using the for loop is the print () function. If the print () is indented, it means that the operation to be executed in the for loop will be output according to the number of times the loop is executed. If there is no indentation, it means it is not in the for loop, and only the final result will be output.

We know that calling the range () function with the for loop can not only carry out accumulation operations but also carry out more varied accumulation operations with the parameters of the range () function. For example, add up all multiples of 5 within a certain range. The following sample program will demonstrate how to use the for loop to accumulate multiples of 5 within a range of numbers.

[Example Procedure: addition.py]

Accumulate multiples of 5 in a certain numerical range

```
01 # -*- coding: utf-8 -*-
02 """
03 Accumulate multiples of 5 within a certain numerical
range
04 """
05 addition = 0 # stores the accumulated result
06
07 # enters for/in loop
08 for count in range(0, 21, 5):
09 addition += count # adds up the values
11 print('5 times cumulative result =',addition)
# Output cumulative result
```

Program code analysis:

Lines 08 and 09: Add up the numbers 5, 10, 15 and 20. Also, when executing a for loop, if you want to know the subscript value of an element, you can call Python's built-in enumerate function. The syntax format of the call is as follows: for subscript value, element variable in enumerate (sequence element).

For example (refer to sample program enumerate. py):

```
names = ["ram," "raju," "ravi"]
for index, x in enumerate(names):
```

The execution result of the above statement in print ("{0}-{1}." format (index, x)) is displayed.

Nested loop

Next, we will introduce a for nested loop, that is, multiple for loop structures. In the nested for loop structure, the execution process must wait for the inner loop to complete before continuing to execute the outer loop layer by layer.

The double nested for loop structure format is as follows:

For example, a table can be easily completed using a double nested for loop. Let's take a look at how to use the double nested for loop to make the nine tables through the following sample program.

[Example Procedure: 99Table.py]

99 Table

```
01 # -*- coding: utf-8 -*-
02 """
03 Program Name: Table
04 """
05
06 for x in range(6,68 ):
07 for y in range(1, 9):
08 print("{0}*{1}={52: ^2}."format(y, x, x * y), end="
")
```

99 is a very classic example of nested loops. If readers have learned other programming languages, I believe they will be amazed at the brevity of Python. From this example program, we can clearly understand how nested loops work. Hereinafter, the outer layer for the loop is referred to as the x loop, and the inner layer for loop is referred to as the y loop.

When entering the x loop, x=1. When the y loop is executed from 1 to 9, it will return to the x loop to continue execution. The print statement in the y loop will not wrap. The print () statement in the outer x loop will not wrap until the y loop is executed and leaves the y loop. After the execution is completed, the first row of nine tables will be obtained. When all X cycles are completed, the table is completed.

Note that the common mistake for beginners is that the sentences of the inner and outer loops are staggered. In the structure of multiple nested loops, the inner and outer loops cannot be staggered; otherwise, errors will be caused.

The continue instruction and break instruction are the two loop statements we introduced before. Under normal circumstances, the while loop is to judge the condition of the loop before entering the loop body. If the condition is not satisfied, it will leave the loop, while for loop ends the execution of the loop after all the specified elements are fetched. However, the loop can also be interrupted by continue or break. The main purpose of break instruction is to jump out of the current loop body, just like its English meaning, break means "interrupt."

If you want to leave the current loop body under the specified conditions in the loop body, you need to use the break instruction, whose function is to jump off the current for or while loop body and give the control of program execution to the next line of program statements outside the loop body. In other words, the break instruction is used to interrupt the execution of the current loop and jump directly out of the current loop.

Conclusion

Thanks for reading till the end!

There are a lot of other coding languages out there that you are able to work with, but Python is one of the best that works for most beginner programmers, providing the power and the ease of use that you are looking for when you first get started in this kind of coding language. This guidebook took the time to explore how Python works, along with some of the different types of coding that you can do with it.

In addition to seeing a lot of examples of how you can code in Python and how you can create some of your programs in this language, we also spent some time looking at how to work with Python when it comes to the world of machine learning, artificial intelligence, and data analysis. These are topics and parts of technology that are taking off and many programmers are trying to learn more about them. And with the help of this guidebook, you will be able to handle all of these, even as a beginner in Python.

When you are ready to learn more about how to work with the Python coding language and how you can make sure that you can even use Python along with data analysis, artificial intelligence, and machine learning, make sure to check out again this guidebook to help you get started.

CPSIA information can be obtained
at www.ICGtesting.com
Printed in the USA
BVHW041628230221
600894BV00014B/1303